The Middle Earth LEGO Minifigure Catalog

From The Hobbit To Lord of The Rings

Christoph Bartneck

First Edition

Dr. Christoph Bartneck is an associate professor at the University of Canterbury, New Zealand. He worked for the LEGO Group in Billund in the 90s, which reignited his passion for LEGO. Since then, he worked in the USA, Netherlands, Japan and now in New Zealand as a researcher and designer. His research focuses on anthropomorphism in robots and figures and his research has been published in acknowledge scientific journals and books.

Copyright by Christoph Bartneck
Christchurch, New Zealand
http://www.minifigure.org

Version 1.0, printed in 2016 by CreateSpace
ISBN-13: 978-1535193429
ISBN-10: 1535193425

A catalogue record for this book is available from the National Library of New Zealand.

Table of contents

iv

Also available:

The
Unofficial
LEGO®
Minifigure
Catalog
2nd Edition

The
2011
LEGO®
Minifigure
Catalog
2nd Edition

The
2012
LEGO®
Minifigure
Catalog
2nd Edition

The
2013
LEGO®
Minifigure
Catalog
2nd Edition

The
2014
LEGO®
Minifigure
Catalog
2nd Edition

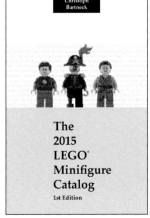

The
2015
LEGO®
Minifigure
Catalog
1st Edition

Introduction

John Ronald Reuel Tolkien's books have inspired generations of readers and movie goers. The LEGO company wisely licensed this work in 2012 when the first of Peter Jackson's movies appeared. The 40 sets that have appeared since then have been well received and in particular "An Unexpected Gathering" 79003 is one of the best sets the LEGO company ever produced. But Tolkien's work did not only appear in sets, it was also featured in several LEGO computer games that are among the stronger titles of TT Games Publishing.

With the completion of both movie triologies only a few more Minifigures in this theme were produced, mainly within the Dimensions theme. This line of products is well known for hosting a wide variety of characters from different franchises. So there is hope for yet another Gandalf or Frodo.

Minifigure Nomenclature

The nomenclature is based on the three levels of themes and the inclusion of the year. Each theme received a three letter code, listed at http://www.minifigure-org/taxonomy/, which already includes the codes for even non-standard scale Minifigures. This resolved the need to distinguish between, for example, the City Minifigures and the Town Minifigures. All the figures in the Town precede the figures from the City theme. The nomenclature for Minifigures used in this book is:

hhh.mmm.lll.yyyy.ss

where:

h denotes the high-level theme
m denotes the mid-level theme
l denotes the low-level theme
y denotes the year in which the figure was first released
s denotes a serial number

Price Guide

The price guide lists the average price for which each Minifigure was traded on-Bricklink during the period of September 2015-February 2016 in USD. I included prices for both new and used Minifigures, if available.

More Information

If you want to know more about the other Minifigures the LEGO produced then please consider looking at The Unofficial LEGO Minifigure Catalog. You might also be interested in the non-standard scale LEGO figures, which is published in The Complete LEGO Figure Catalog. Both books are available from Amazon.com and other retailers.

I included QR code in the book for the first time. You can use our Minifigure app on your phone to scan the code which will take you directly to the respective Minifigure entry. Get the App now!

Licensed

Middle Earth

Lord Of The Rings

Gandalf the Grey

lic.mea.lor.2012.01

Bricklink	lor001	
# Parts	6	
Price New	4.10	
Price Used	2.99	
Head	3626cpb0729	
Sets	79003-1, 9469-1, 30213-1, 79010-1	

Frodo Baggins

lic.mea.lor.2012.02

Bricklink	lor002	
# Parts	4	
Price New	3.90	
Price Used	2.61	
Head	3626cpb0730	
Sets	30210-1, 9469-1	

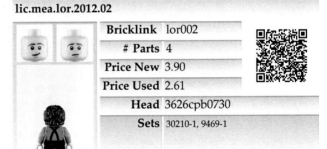

Frodo Baggins

lic.mea.lor.2012.03

Bricklink	lor003	
# Parts	5	
Price New	7.06	
Price Used	4.34	
Head	3626cpb0728	
Sets	9470-1	

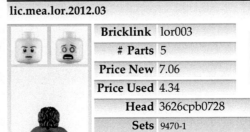

Samwise Gamgee

lic.mea.lor.2012.04

Bricklink	lor004	
# Parts	5	
Price New	23.48	
Price Used	18.61	
Head	3626cpb0758	
Sets	9470-1	

Gollum

lic.mea.lor.2012.05

Bricklink	lor005	
# Parts	3	
Price New	8.69	
Price Used	5.72	
Head		
Sets	9470-1	

Uruk-hai

lic.mea.lor.2012.06

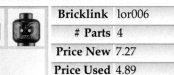

Bricklink	lor006	
# Parts	4	
Price New	7.27	
Price Used	4.89	
Head	3626cpb0719	
Sets	9471-1	

Uruk-hai

lic.mea.lor.2012.07

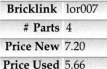

Bricklink	lor007	
# Parts	4	
Price New	7.20	
Price Used	5.66	
Head	3626cpb0719	
Sets	9474-1, 9471-1	

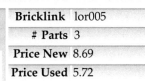

Uruk-hai

lic.mea.lor.2012.08

Bricklink	lor008
# Parts	5
Price New	8.61
Price Used	6.84
Head	3626cpb0719
Sets	9474-1, 9471-1, 30211-1

Rohan Soldier

lic.mea.lor.2012.09

Bricklink	lor009
# Parts	5
Price New	18.33
Price Used	16.23
Head	3626cpb0724
Sets	9471-1

Eomer

lic.mea.lor.2012.10

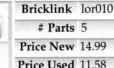

Bricklink	lor010
# Parts	5
Price New	14.99
Price Used	11.58
Head	3626cpb0725
Sets	9471-1

Moria Orc

lic.mea.lor.2012.11

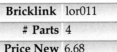

Bricklink	lor011
# Parts	4
Price New	6.68
Price Used	5.36
Head	3626cpb0731
Sets	9473-1

Pippin

lic.mea.lor.2012.12

Bricklink	lor012
# Parts	5
Price New	21.56
Price Used	16.65
Head	3626cpb0732
Sets	9473-1

Gimli

lic.mea.lor.2012.13

Bricklink	lor013
# Parts	5
Price New	4.99
Price Used	4.14
Head	3626cpb0733
Sets	79008-1, 9474-1, 79006-1, 9473-1

Boromir

lic.mea.lor.2012.14

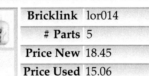

Bricklink	lor014
# Parts	5
Price New	18.45
Price Used	15.06
Head	3626cpb0734
Sets	9473-1

Legolas

lic.mea.lor.2012.15

Bricklink	lor015
# Parts	4
Price New	9.88
Price Used	9.05
Head	3626cpb0735
Sets	79008-1, 9473-1

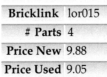

Merry

lic.mea.lor.2012.16

Bricklink	lor016
# Parts	5
Price New	20.73
Price Used	17.23
Head	3626cpb0726
Sets	9472-1

Aragorn

lic.mea.lor.2012.17

Bricklink	lor017
# Parts	4
Price New	6.66
Price Used	5.19
Head	3626cpb0727
Sets	9472-1, 79008-1, 9474-1

Ringwraith

lic.mea.lor.2012.18

Bricklink	lor018
# Parts	5
Price New	15.53
Price Used	13.38
Head	3626b
Sets	9472-1

Uruk-hai

lic.mea.lor.2012.19

Bricklink	lor019
# Parts	3
Price New	6.35
Price Used	5.77
Head	3626cpb0759
Sets	9474-1

Haldir

lic.mea.lor.2012.20

Bricklink	lor020
# Parts	5
Price New	19.28
Price Used	16.55
Head	3626cpb0753
Sets	9474-1

King Theoden

lic.mea.lor.2012.21

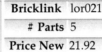

Bricklink	lor021
# Parts	5
Price New	21.92
Price Used	15.39
Head	3626cpb0754
Sets	9474-1

Uruk-hai

lic.mea.lor.2012.22

Bricklink	lor022
# Parts	5
Price New	12.93
Price Used	10.25
Head	3626cpb0719
Sets	9476-1, 10237-1

Mordor Orc

lic.mea.lor.2012.23

Bricklink	lor023
# Parts	4
Price New	7.11
Price Used	6.09
Head	3626cpb0720
Sets	9476-1

Mordor Orc

lic.mea.lor.2012.24

Bricklink	lor024
# Parts	3
Price New	4.17
Price Used	3.38
Head	3626cpb0720
Sets	79007-1, 79008-1, 9476-1, 10237-1

Lurtz

lic.mea.lor.2012.25

Bricklink	lor025
# Parts	4
Price New	7.43
Price Used	6.82
Head	3626cpb0718
Sets	9476-1

Cave Troll

lic.mea.lor.2012.26

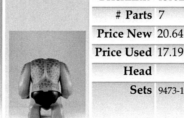

Bricklink	lor027
# Parts	7
Price New	20.64
Price Used	17.19
Head	
Sets	9473-1

Frodo Baggins

lic.mea.lor.2012.27

Bricklink	lor028
# Parts	5
Price New	5.64
Price Used	4.07
Head	3626cpb0728
Sets	9472-1

Elrond

lic.mea.lor.2012.28

Bricklink	lor033
# Parts	5
Price New	17.74
Price Used	16.19
Head	3626bpb0811
Sets	5000202-1

Saruman

lic.mea.lor.2013.01

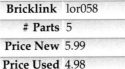

Bricklink	lor058
# Parts	5
Price New	5.99
Price Used	4.98
Head	3626cpb0938
Sets	79005-1

Elrond

lic.mea.lor.2013.02

Bricklink	lor059
# Parts	5
Price New	6.37
Price Used	4.80
Head	3626cpb0939
Sets	79006-1

Arwen

lic.mea.lor.2013.03

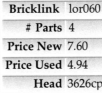

Bricklink	lor060
# Parts	4
Price New	7.60
Price Used	4.94
Head	3626cpb0936
Sets	79006-1

Gandalf the Grey

lic.mea.lor.2013.04

Bricklink	lor061
# Parts	5
Price New	3.02
Price Used	2.37
Head	3626cpb0937
Sets	79005-1

Frodo Baggins

lic.mea.lor.2013.05

Bricklink	lor062
# Parts	4
Price New	3.27
Price Used	2.70
Head	3626cpb0947
Sets	79006-1

Gandalf the White

lic.mea.lor.2013.06

Bricklink	lor063
# Parts	5
Price New	8.94
Price Used	5.82
Head	3626cpb0937
Sets	79007-1

Mouth of Sauron

lic.mea.lor.2013.07

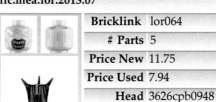

Bricklink	lor064
# Parts	5
Price New	11.75
Price Used	7.94
Head	3626cpb0948
Sets	79007-1

Mordor Orc

lic.mea.lor.2013.08

Bricklink	lor065
# Parts	4
Price New	5.54
Price Used	3.84
Head	3626cpb0720
Sets	79007-1

Aragorn

lic.mea.lor.2013.09

Bricklink	lor066
# Parts	5
Price New	8.51
Price Used	6.52
Head	3626cpb0727
Sets	79007-1

Pirate of Umbar

lic.mea.lor.2013.10

Bricklink	lor067
# Parts	4
Price New	5.81
Price Used	5.42
Head	3626cpb0952
Sets	79008-1

Mordor Orc

lic.mea.lor.2013.11

Bricklink	lor068
# Parts	4
Price New	5.27
Price Used	4.05
Head	3626cpb0720
Sets	79008-1

Soldier of the Dead

lic.mea.lor.2013.12

Bricklink	lor069
# Parts	5
Price New	12.88
Price Used	9.72
Head	3626cpb0950
Sets	79008-1

Soldier of the Dead

lic.mea.lor.2013.13

Bricklink	lor070
# Parts	5
Price New	12.72
Price Used	9.88
Head	3626cpb0950
Sets	79008-1

King of the Dead

lic.mea.lor.2013.14

Bricklink	lor071
# Parts	5
Price New	10.72
Price Used	10.07
Head	3626cpb0951
Sets	79008-1

Grima Wormtongue

lic.mea.lor.2013.15

Bricklink	lor072
# Parts	5
Price New	17.49
Price Used	14.33
Head	3626cpb0949
Sets	10237-1

Gandalf the Grey

lic.mea.lor.2013.16

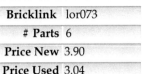

Bricklink	lor073
# Parts	6
Price New	3.90
Price Used	3.04
Head	3626cpb0937
Sets	79014-1, 10237-1

Saruman

lic.mea.lor.2013.17

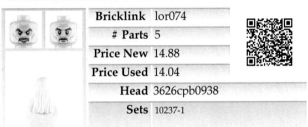

Bricklink	lor074
# Parts	5
Price New	14.88
Price Used	14.04
Head	3626cpb0938
Sets	10237-1

Middle Earth

Other

Gandalf

lic.mea.oth.2015.01

Bricklink	dim001
# Parts	6
Price New	7.91
Price Used	7.74
Head	3626cpb1430
Sets	6107300-1

Gimli

lic.mea.oth.2015.02

Bricklink	dim007
# Parts	5
Price New	
Price Used	5.79
Head	3626cpb1435
Sets	71220-1

Legolas

lic.mea.oth.2015.03

Bricklink	dim008
# Parts	4
Price New	6.90
Price Used	5.56
Head	3626cpb0812
Sets	71219-1

Middle Earth

The Hobbit

Mirkwood Elf Guard

lic.mea.hob.2012.01

Bricklink	lor026
# Parts	5
Price New	8.55
Price Used	6.54
Head	3626cpb0753
Sets	30212-1

Bilbo Baggins

lic.mea.hob.2012.02

Bricklink	lor029
# Parts	4
Price New	5.01
Price Used	4.31
Head	3626cpb0872
Sets	79003-1

Bilbo Baggins

lic.mea.hob.2012.03

Bricklink	lor030
# Parts	4
Price New	3.90
Price Used	2.96
Head	3626cpb0818
Sets	79004-1, 79013-1, comcon033-1, 79000-1

Gollum

lic.mea.hob.2012.04

Bricklink	lor031
# Parts	3
Price New	6.57
Price Used	4.08
Head	
Sets	79000-1

Goblin Soldier

lic.mea.hob.2012.05

Bricklink	lor032
# Parts	4
Price New	5.82
Price Used	4.82
Head	3626cpb0871
Sets	79010-1

Tauriel

lic.mea.hob.2012.06

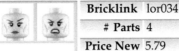

Bricklink	lor034
# Parts	4
Price New	5.79
Price Used	5.12
Head	3626cpb0813
Sets	79001-1

Legolas Greenleaf

lic.mea.hob.2012.07

Bricklink	lor035
# Parts	4
Price New	5.14
Price Used	4.91
Head	3626cpb0812
Sets	79001-1

Fili the Dwarf

lic.mea.hob.2012.08

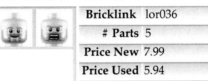
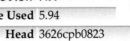

Bricklink	lor036
# Parts	5
Price New	7.99
Price Used	5.94
Head	3626cpb0823
Sets	79001-1

Kili the Dwarf

lic.mea.hob.2012.09

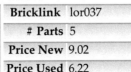

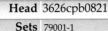

Bricklink	lor037
# Parts	5
Price New	9.02
Price Used	6.22
Head	3626cpb0821
Sets	79001-1

Yazneg

lic.mea.hob.2012.10

Bricklink	lor038
# Parts	4
Price New	3.61
Price Used	2.57
Head	3626cpb0816
Sets	79002-1

Hunter Orc

lic.mea.hob.2012.11

Bricklink	lor039
# Parts	4
Price New	5.17
Price Used	3.91
Head	3626bpb0720
Sets	79002-1

Thorin Oakenshield

lic.mea.hob.2012.12

Bricklink	lor040
# Parts	4
Price New	10.36
Price Used	7.60
Head	3626cpb0814
Sets	79002-1

Bifur the Dwarf

lic.mea.hob.2012.13

Bricklink	lor041
# Parts	5
Price New	7.50
Price Used	6.13
Head	3626cpb0815
Sets	79002-1

Goblin King

lic.mea.hob.2012.14

Bricklink	lor042	
# Parts	10	
Price New	11.13	
Price Used	10.55	
Head		
Sets	79010-1	

Goblin Soldier

lic.mea.hob.2012.15

Bricklink	lor043	
# Parts	4	
Price New	5.78	
Price Used	4.45	
Head	3626cpb0871	
Sets	79010-1	

Goblin Scribe

lic.mea.hob.2012.16

Bricklink	lor044	
# Parts	4	
Price New	4.95	
Price Used	3.87	
Head	3626cpb0871	
Sets	79010-1	

Ori the Dwarf

lic.mea.hob.2012.17

Bricklink	lor045	
# Parts	5	
Price New	16.13	
Price Used	14.45	
Head	3626cpb0836	
Sets	79010-1	

Nori the Dwarf

lic.mea.hob.2012.18

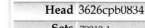

Bricklink	lor046
# Parts	4
Price New	18.99
Price Used	16.48
Head	3626cpb0834
Sets	79010-1

Dori the Dwarf

lic.mea.hob.2012.19

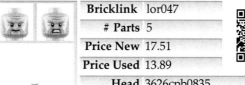

Bricklink	lor047
# Parts	5
Price New	17.51
Price Used	13.89
Head	3626cpb0835
Sets	79010-1

Hunter Orc

lic.mea.hob.2012.20

Bricklink	lor048
# Parts	5
Price New	5.35
Price Used	4.39
Head	3626bpb0720
Sets	79002-1

Balin the Dwarf

lic.mea.hob.2012.21

Bricklink	lor049
# Parts	5
Price New	8.48
Price Used	6.48
Head	3626cpb0866
Sets	79003-1

Dwalin the Dwarf

lic.mea.hob.2012.22

Bricklink	lor050
# Parts	5
Price New	8.69
Price Used	7.55
Head	3626cpb0867
Sets	79003-1

Bombur the Dwarf

lic.mea.hob.2012.23

Bricklink	lor051
# Parts	4
Price New	10.01
Price Used	8.17
Head	3626cpb0868
Sets	79003-1

Bofur the Dwarf

lic.mea.hob.2012.24

Bricklink	lor052
# Parts	5
Price New	12.47
Price Used	10.24
Head	3626cpb0869
Sets	79003-1

Mirkwood Elf Guard

lic.mea.hob.2012.25

Bricklink	lor053
# Parts	4
Price New	5.85
Price Used	3.81
Head	3626cpb0753
Sets	79004-1

Mirkwood Elf Chief

lic.mea.hob.2012.26

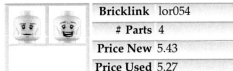

Bricklink	lor054
# Parts	4
Price New	5.43
Price Used	5.27
Head	3626cpb0822
Sets	79004-1

Gloin the Dwarf

lic.mea.hob.2012.27

Bricklink	lor055
# Parts	4
Price New	13.45
Price Used	12.69
Head	3626cpb0819
Sets	79004-1

Oin the Dwarf

lic.mea.hob.2012.28

Bricklink	lor056
# Parts	5
Price New	12.54
Price Used	10.18
Head	3626cpb0820
Sets	79004-1

Bilbo Baggins

lic.mea.hob.2013.01

Bricklink	lor057
# Parts	4
Price New	74.70
Price Used	118.90
Head	3626cpb0818
Sets	LOTRDVDBD

Beorn

lic.mea.hob.2013.02

Bricklink	lor075
# Parts	3
Price New	4.79
Price Used	3.35
Head	
Sets	79011-1

Gundabad Orc

lic.mea.hob.2013.03

Bricklink	lor076
# Parts	4
Price New	4.38
Price Used	2.93
Head	3626cpb1016
Sets	79011-1

Gundabad Orc

lic.mea.hob.2013.04

Bricklink	lor077
# Parts	5
Price New	4.70
Price Used	3.61
Head	3626cpb1016
Sets	79011-1

Mirkwood Elf Archer

lic.mea.hob.2013.05

Bricklink	lor078
# Parts	5
Price New	4.82
Price Used	4.41
Head	3626cpb0753
Sets	79012-1

Thranduil

lic.mea.hob.2013.06

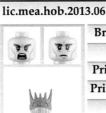

Bricklink	lor079
# Parts	5
Price New	5.92
Price Used	5.78
Head	3626cpb1021
Sets	79012-1

Mirkwood Elf

lic.mea.hob.2013.07

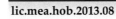

Bricklink	lor080
# Parts	4
Price New	4.35
Price Used	4.45
Head	3626cpb0753
Sets	79012-1

Necromancer of Dol Guldur

lic.mea.hob.2013.08

Bricklink	lor081
# Parts	3
Price New	5.12
Price Used	4.19
Head	3626cpb1019
Sets	79014-1

Radagast

lic.mea.hob.2013.09

Bricklink	lor082
# Parts	6
Price New	12.64
Price Used	10.05
Head	3626cpb1020
Sets	79014-1

Thorin Oakenshield

lic.mea.hob.2013.10

Bricklink	lor083
# Parts	4
Price New	6.70
Price Used	5.64
Head	3626cpb0814
Sets	79013-1

Bard the Bowman

lic.mea.hob.2013.11

Bricklink	lor084
# Parts	4
Price New	6.22
Price Used	6.31
Head	3626cpb1022
Sets	79013-1

Master of Lake-town

lic.mea.hob.2013.12

Bricklink	lor085
# Parts	6
Price New	8.05
Price Used	8.06
Head	3626cpb1023
Sets	79013-1

Lake-town Guard

lic.mea.hob.2013.13

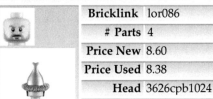

Bricklink	lor086
# Parts	4
Price New	8.60
Price Used	8.38
Head	3626cpb1024
Sets	79013-1

Azog

lic.mea.hob.2013.14

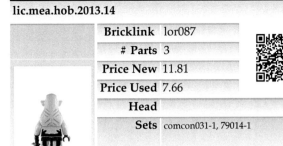

Bricklink	lor087
# Parts	3
Price New	11.81
Price Used	7.66
Head	
Sets	comcon031-1, 79014-1

Gundabad Orc

lic.mea.hob.2013.15

Bricklink	lor088
# Parts	3
Price New	3.28
Price Used	2.29
Head	3626cpb1016
Sets	79014-1, 79012-1

Gundabad Orc

lic.mea.hob.2013.16

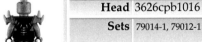

Bricklink	lor089
# Parts	4
Price New	3.89
Price Used	3.34
Head	3626cpb1016
Sets	79014-1, 79012-1

Statue at Dol Guldur

lic.mea.hob.2013.17

Bricklink	lor090
# Parts	3
Price New	4.31
Price Used	3.23
Head	3626b-3
Sets	79014-1

Bilbo Baggins

lic.mea.hob.2014.01

Bricklink	lor091
# Parts	4
Price New	14.22
Price Used	12.26
Head	3626cpb0872
Sets	5002130-1

Bard the Bowman

lic.mea.hob.2014.02

Bricklink	lor092
# Parts	4
Price New	5.21
Price Used	7.11
Head	3626cpb1022
Sets	comcon038-1, 79017-1

Bilbo Baggins

lic.mea.hob.2014.03

Bricklink	lor093
# Parts	4
Price New	7.36
Price Used	5.87
Head	3626cpb0818
Sets	79018-1

Balin the Dwarf

lic.mea.hob.2014.04

Bricklink	lor094
# Parts	4
Price New	7.06
Price Used	
Head	3626cpb0866
Sets	79018-1

Dwalin the Dwarf

lic.mea.hob.2014.05

Bricklink	lor095
# Parts	4
Price New	7.32
Price Used	
Head	3626cpb0867
Sets	79018-1

Kili the Dwarf

lic.mea.hob.2014.06

Bricklink	lor096
# Parts	4
Price New	7.81
Price Used	
Head	3626cpb0821
Sets	79018-1, col12-11

Fili the Dwarf

lic.mea.hob.2014.07

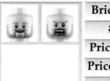

Bricklink	lor097
# Parts	4
Price New	7.21
Price Used	
Head	3626cpb0823
Sets	79018-1

Tauriel

lic.mea.hob.2014.08

Bricklink	lor098
# Parts	4
Price New	5.38
Price Used	
Head	3626cpb0813
Sets	79016-1

Bard the Bowman

lic.mea.hob.2014.09

Bricklink	lor099
# Parts	4
Price New	4.98
Price Used	4.11
Head	3626cpb1197
Sets	79016-1

Bain Son of Bard

lic.mea.hob.2014.10

Bricklink	lor100
# Parts	4
Price New	4.37
Price Used	3.44
Head	3626cpb1198
Sets	79016-1

Hunter Orc

lic.mea.hob.2014.11

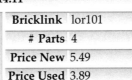

Bricklink	lor101
# Parts	4
Price New	5.49
Price Used	3.89
Head	3626cpb1199
Sets	79016-1

Hunter Orc

lic.mea.hob.2014.12

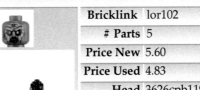

Bricklink	lor102
# Parts	5
Price New	5.60
Price Used	4.83
Head	3626cpb1199
Sets	79016-1

Galadriel

lic.mea.hob.2014.13

Bricklink	lor103
# Parts	5
Price New	5.31
Price Used	4.75
Head	3626cpb1201
Sets	79015-1

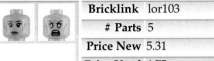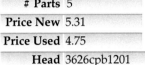

Witch-King

lic.mea.hob.2014.14

Bricklink	lor104
# Parts	5
Price New	5.19
Price Used	4.84
Head	3626cpb1202
Sets	79015-1

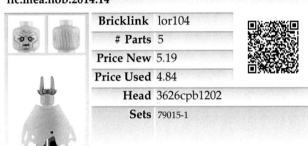

Elrond

lic.mea.hob.2014.15

Bricklink	lor105
# Parts	5
Price New	5.17
Price Used	4.75
Head	3626cpb0939
Sets	79015-1

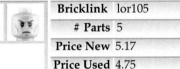

Thorin Oakenshield

lic.mea.hob.2014.16

Bricklink	lor106
# Parts	4
Price New	9.88
Price Used	6.33
Head	3626cpb0814
Sets	79017-1

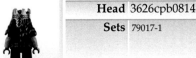

Dain Ironfoot

lic.mea.hob.2014.17

Bricklink	lor107
# Parts	5
Price New	11.77
Price Used	9.86
Head	3626cpb0819
Sets	79017-1

Azog

lic.mea.hob.2014.18

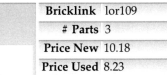

Bricklink	lor109
# Parts	3
Price New	10.18
Price Used	8.23
Head	
Sets	79017-1

Gundabad Orc

lic.mea.hob.2014.19

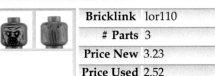

Bricklink	lor110
# Parts	3
Price New	3.23
Price Used	2.52
Head	3626cpb1205
Sets	79017-1

Bain Son of Bard

lic.mea.hob.2015.01

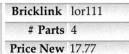

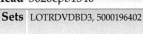

Bricklink	lor111
# Parts	4
Price New	17.77
Price Used	18.91
Head	3626cpb1340
Sets	LOTRDVDBD3, 5000196402

Made in the USA
San Bernardino, CA
22 April 2019